ß

FEB 2 1 2007

Holidays and Celebrations in Colonial America

Mitchell Lane
PUBLISHERS

P.O. Box 196 • Hockessin, Delaware 19707

B

Titles in the Series

Holidays and Celebrations in Colonial America

Russell Roberts

Copyright © 2007 by Mitchell Lane Publishers, Inc. All rights reserved. No part of this book may be reproduced without written permission from the publisher. Printed and bound in the United States of America.

Printing   1   2   3   4   5   6   7   8   9

Library of Congress Cataloging-in-Publication Data
Roberts, Russell, 1953–
    Holidays and celebrations in colonial America / by Russell Roberts.
        p. cm.—(Building America)
    Includes bibliographical references and index.
    ISBN 1-58415-467-5 (lib. bdg.)
    1. Holidays—United States—History—Juvenile literature. 2. United States—History—Colonial period, ca. 1600–1775—Juvenile literature. 3. United States—Social life and customs—To 1775—Juvenile literature. I. Title. II. Building America (Hockessin, Del.)
GT4803.R63 2006
394.26973—dc22

                                                                    2005027982

ISBN-10:1-58415-467-5   ISBN-13: 978-1-58415-467-9

ABOUT THE AUTHOR: Russell Roberts has written and published nearly 40 books for adults and children on a variety of subjects, including baseball, memory power, business, New Jersey history, and travel. The lives of American figures of distinction is a particular area of interest for him. He has written numerous books for Mitchell Lane Publishers, including *Pedro Menendez de Aviles*, *Philo Farnsworth Invents TV*, *Robert Goddard*, *Bernardo de Galvez*, and *Where Did the Dinosaurs Go?* He lives in Bordentown, New Jersey, with his family and a fat, fuzzy, and crafty calico cat named Rusti.

PHOTO CREDITS: Cover, pp. 1, 3, 6, 36, 38—North Wind Picture Archives; p. 10—*Harper's Weekly*; pp. 12—Stock Montage/Getty Images; pp. 15, 18, 21, 41—Library of Congress; p. 26—Keystone/Getty Images; p. 28—British Library; p. 40—Hulton Archive/Getty Images.

PUBLISHER'S NOTE: This story is based on the author's extensive research, which he believes to be accurate. Documentation of such research is contained on page 46.
    The internet sites referenced herein were active as of the publication date. Due to the fleeting nature of some web sites, we cannot guarantee they will all be active when you are reading this book.

                                                                    PLB

Contents

*For Your Information

In colonial America, St. Nicholas was believed to travel on a horse. It wasn't until the 1820s, when Clement Clarke Moore published the poem "'Twas the Night Before Christmas," that "eight tiny reindeer" would pull Santa Claus in a sleigh.

Chapter

1

Like Any Other Day

You are a young boy or girl living in New England in colonial America. The American Revolution, and the country that will become the United States of America, is many years in the future.

It is a winter morning. The sun rises late, so the first light doesn't hit your room until 7:00 A.M. or so. However, you were awake much earlier than that, for feeding the chickens and the livestock is one of your jobs and you had to do that before dawn. After feeding the animals you came back into your house and lay down for a few minutes, but now with first light you know sleeping is out of the question. You have many chores to do, and the earlier you start them, the better.

It is late in December—the 25th day of the month, to be exact. It has been cold outside for many weeks now. The cold hugs the floor and lurks in the corners of the large room in which you sleep with your mother and father. The fire in the fireplace never seems to be able to completely chase away the chill.

You think of the date again—December 25—and suddenly remember something. A few weeks ago, a Dutch traveler had come to your house around dusk. He needed food and shelter. Your parents had kindly offered to let him stay there for the night, and he had gladly accepted. He was cold, tired, and hungry.

That night, while you lay in your bed in the corner trying to ignore the biting cold, you listened as the Dutch guest talked to your parents while they all sat around the fireplace after eating. He was telling them about how much he missed being at home in New York City, for it was around the time of Sinterklaas Eve. According to him, Sinterklaas Eve was the start of a joyful holiday season in New York City. The women baked sweet desserts, the men drank and danced, and the children waited anxiously for someone named Sinterklaas. He brought good children presents, like candies and fruit.

The Dutch traveler went on to say that the whole city came alive in an atmosphere of fun and gaiety during this time. Work slowed down, and the people went to parties, visited one another, and otherwise enjoyed themselves. These festivities often lasted until December 25 or later.

In fact, the Dutch guest had said, he knew of some people who celebrated on December 25—a day called Christmas Day. He had been down south one year, in Virginia, and there plantation owners had decorated their homes with pieces of evergreens and holly. They too celebrated this day called Christmas by dancing, singing, playing cards, and feasting. Sometimes the celebrations went on into early January. Holidays, said the guest, are wonderful things.

Father had listened to this account in virtual silence, rocking slowly back and forth in front of the fire, smoking his pipe. Occasionally he interjected a word or two in his deep voice. Mother had listened too as she mended some clothes with her needle and thread. She did not say anything, but then again, she almost never did.

Eventually the adults went to bed (the Dutch guest snored like a man sawing wood!), leaving you with visions of Sinterklaas and Christmas Day and parties and presents dancing in your head. You somewhat understood the concept of a holiday, but you had never experienced one. Sometimes your family got together with others of the community and had a feast. Prayers were said, thanking God for blessing the harvest. That was a holiday, because work for the day was suspended, but it was nothing like what the Dutch traveler had talked about—parties, pastries, and presents.

As the days passed you had forgotten about that. With all the work you had to do around the farm, you had little time for idle thinking. But here it was, December 25, and suddenly you had remembered. Somewhere people were celebrating something called Christmas. Somewhere they were feasting,

In colonial times, Christmas was celebrated in different ways depending upon where one lived. There could be parties, singing, visiting, a
visit from St. Nicholas . . . even a pineapple used as a decoration!

dancing, and singing. Somewhere children were receiving presents of sweets, fruits, and nuts.

You shake your head. What did it matter to you what was happening somewhere else today? It wasn't happening to you. Today, December 25, was just like any other day for you; just like any other day.

People wassailing. The word wassail comes from "waes haeil," which means "good health" or "be well." If you drank from the wassail bowl, you were drinking to someone's health and well being.

Depending on your culture, upbringing, and location, you, as a child living in colonial America, may never have experienced Christmas, even if you were a Christian. Christians didn't automatically celebrate holidays such as Christmas, as they do today. Some people observed the day, and some did not. For those who did not, days like Christmas Day were just like any other day, filled with the same routine of hard work as always.

Holidays—or "holy days," celebrations commemorating a holy event —were not common in colonial America. Many of the holidays celebrated in the settlers' native countries seemed to have become forgotten by people once they arrived in America. As the adventurers came across the ocean in ships, traditions and ceremonies that they had celebrated in the Old World were lost. As one expert noted, "Much was lost in transit. . . . Where were the morris dancers, the wassailing, the annual wakes, the crafts holidays, maypoles? The great bulk of the early migrants dissolved into the farm population."[1]

This was life in colonial America.

Colonial Children

Children in colonial America did not have as much free time as kids do today. However, they also had much more responsibility, and they were sometimes allowed to do things that would horrify modern parents.

From about age three, colonial children were given chores to do. This was done for two reasons: to ensure that they helped in the running of a household, whose survival depended upon everyone doing his or her part; and to keep the children from getting underfoot. Colonial parents had much to do on their own, and little time to worry about entertaining their children. A young girl in 1775 listed twenty-six chores she had accomplished, including sewing, ironing, making a broom, and milking the cows. Toys, particularly in families without much money, were usually homemade.

A child playing with a colonial doll

Boys and girls were treated very differently when it came to schooling. It was considered much more important for girls to learn how to perform household duties than it was for them to attend school. Many girls were married by age sixteen. Boys attended some school, but the amount varied depending upon financial and social status. By age sixteen, boys became taxpayers and were eligible to serve in the militia.

Because their parents were so busy, colonial children spent much of the day unsupervised. This sometimes led to a child doing things on his or her own that seem dangerous to us. For example, future second president John Adams was given a gun at eight years old. He spent hours by himself with the gun, shooting at birds.

In general, colonial children moved briskly on the road to adulthood, without any of the "teenage anguish" so common today. There just wasn't time or energy back then for anyone—kids or their parents—to indulge in any of that.

A woman spins yarn while reading a book. Colonial people had to be as efficient as possible.

Chapter

②

Busy as Bees

Colonial families had so many daily chores to do that they had little time for much else. There were few stores where they could go to buy what they needed. Food, clothing, tools, shelter . . . practically everything had to be grown, made, or built by the settlers themselves.

When colonists needed a hand, they counted on their neighbors for help. Neighbors helping neighbors was the only way to survive in the inhospitable wilderness of early America.

In the isolated environment of colonial America, in which people might go weeks without seeing another person besides the members of their own family, it was only logical that when neighbors did see each other, they combined the work that needed to be done with fun. This was the idea behind the "bee"—a combination of work and play. Colonists knew that once the hard work was finished, they would be able to eat, drink, and socialize with one another.

Bees could be called for virtually any chore. There were bees for fulling (treating wool so that it would not stretch, and making it thicker and warmer), feather-stripping (producing material for stuffing beds, pillows, and quilts), sewing, spinning (spinning fibers into thread), slaughtering cattle, cutting rags for quilts, and tackling many other jobs.

Land Clearing Bees

Clearing land was usually necessary to build a cabin for new settlers, as well as to plant crops. When a family arrived in an area that had previously been uninhabited, land had to be cleared of trees and brush.

A land clearing bee was sometimes called a chopping bee. In Vermont, it was called a mowing bee. It was not unusual for the colonists to clear from five to eight acres of land at one bee.

Sometimes, the colonists might hold what was called a piling bee. At this bee, people removed tree stumps still in the ground. In New England, the soil was often full of stones and large rocks that needed to be hauled away. The settler would then call a stone-hauling or stone bee.

Barn and House Raisings

One of the most festive occasions at which people helped one another was a barn raising. A barn was an important building for the colonial farmer. It housed animals, tools, feed, carriages, and a multitude of other items. A barn raising was hard work. It usually started early in the morning and continued well into the day. A house raising was similar to a barn raising.

After the work was finally done, the settlers were ready for an evening of food and fun. The dinner menu might include roasted rabbit, squirrel, turkey, deer, or any other type of available game, along with whatever vegetables were in season. Dessert consisted of corn bread, cookies, gingerbread, pie, and baked puddings.

If the house raising was in the South, the menu might feature fried chicken, ham, sweet potatoes, buttered hominy grits, peas, tomatoes, green beans, and biscuits with gravy, along with molasses, coffee, pies, and cakes.

Drink flowed freely at these bees. Men usually drank toasts to the new house or barn, to America, and to each other. A fiddler would often seem to pop up, and the settlers would dance to tunes like "Yankee Doodle" and "The Liberty Song." In regions where musical instruments were not allowed because of religious or cultural reasons, people sang songs without accompaniment.

Games were often part of the celebration. The settlers participated in wrestling matches, pitching horseshoes, target shooting, footraces, and distance jumping.

A barn dance was an event greatly anticipated by both men and women, for it was one of the main occasions for courting, or finding a spouse. They were originally called "bran" dances because grain kernels—in the case of a barn raising, corn kernels—were thrown onto the rough new floor. The dancers' feet would push oil out of the kernels. This oil smoothed and polished the new wood.

Food Preparation Bees

Husking corn was a tedious job. Cornhusking bees were held to husk corn in the shortest amount of time. Neighbors met around a long table piled high with corn ears that had just been picked. They formed two teams. The object was to finish husking all the corn on your side of the table first. As

Although this barn raising took place in more modern times, the idea of friends helping friends has not changed. First the walls are built on the ground. Then they are raised into position. Finally, the roof is added.

they husked, the colonials would talk, joke, and sing. If a young man found a red ear of corn, he was permitted to kiss a girl. If a girl found a red ear, she could hand it to her favorite young man and receive a kiss from him. Married people kissed their spouses. Some crafty single young men would hide a red ear in their pocket before going "a-husking" to ensure the chance to kiss a girl. After the husking dinner, games and contests took place: running and jumping races and "throwing the hammer"—seeing who could throw a hammer the farthest.

Apples were another important food for early Americans. Settlers liked apples because of their versatility. The fruit could be eaten raw, baked, stewed, or made into cider or vinegar. People would get together to pare and cut apples for the winter. These were called apple parings, apple cuts, or apple bees. Sometimes men and women took part in apple bees, and sometimes it was only the women. The ladies shared stories, recipes, songs, and common problems as they worked, tossing peels and fruit into separate pans and baskets. Young girls tried to skin whole apples in a single peel. A girl would fling the curly peel over her left shoulder. A peel that landed unbroken was thought to form the first initial of the girl's future husband.

Sugaring off was another cause for celebration. Native Americans pioneered the production of maple sugar from the sap of maple trees. It became an important household sweetener in the northern colonies. Sugaring off celebrated the production of the first batch of maple sugar from sap. It also signaled the beginning of spring.

Quilting Bees

Quilting bees let women socialize and use their artistic and sewing skills. Often, a quilting bee was the only social activity for women during the long winter months. Quilting bees started early in the morning and lasted most of the day, although they could go longer. One quilting bee in 1752 lasted ten days.

The women would arrive at the bee carrying heaps of rags to add to the quilt. Every fabric scrap that a housewife had was used. Neighbors frequently traded squares of material to get a desired pattern or color.

The men would come by late in the day and eat supper with the women. Then they would play games. One game involved putting the quilt around people's heads and letting them try to find other people in the room. Another was to wrap children and lighter guests in the quilt and then toss them into the air to test the quilt's strength.

Moonlight Work

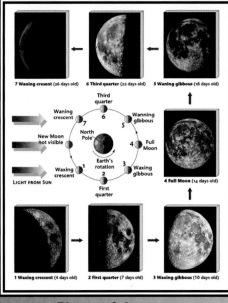

Phases of the moon

Without the benefits of modern conveniences, colonial farmers had to take advantage of whatever was available to get a job done. This included something that is taken for granted in modern times: moonlight.

Moonlight was used in a variety of ways. Farmers who were planning to drive their cattle to market often scheduled the trip for full moon periods so that they could use the bright moonlight to move at night. The same was true of farm chores. Many were done entirely at night, under the light of the full moon, rather than in the heat of day. In winter, farmers were advised to bring produce to market during the bright light of the gibbous moon of January.

Colonial farmers also used the moon as an indicator of when to cut wood. They were told never to cut a tree for wood during a full moon.

Farmers also used the moon as a planting guide. As the moon went through its phases before reaching a full moon (known as a waxing moon), the farmer would plant aboveground crops such as grain and tomatoes. The peak time for planting was considered to be the days just before the full moon. After the full moon, as the moon was going through its phases before it became a new moon (known as a waning moon), the farmer would plant underground or root crops such as carrots.

People's eyes were more accustomed to darkness centuries ago, when no artificial lighting was available. That's a big reason farmers were able to perform difficult chores at night. The colonial farmers' use of moonlight shows their resourcefulness. They would use whatever nature made available to help them survive.

In European countries, people often danced around the maypole to celebrate May Day on May 1. However, the practice was only occasionally followed in colonial America.

Chapter

3

Holidays from January to June

In colonial America, one of the major holidays of the year was New Year's Day. Most other holidays in the months from January to June revolved around the Christian religious holidays that occurred near Easter, such as Shrove Tuesday, Maundy Thursday, and Good Friday. The emphasis on these holidays probably occurred because many of the European immigrants who came to colonial America were Christian. However, some other holidays based on folklore and superstition, such as Candlemas Day and May Day, were also celebrated—although sometimes without the same enthusiasm with which they had been observed in Europe.

New Year's Day

In colonial America, January 1, New Year's Day, was a major holiday. A popular way to celebrate the passing of one year into the next was to hold open houses and go visiting.

Calling on friends on New Year's Day is a custom supposedly started by the Chinese. In colonial New York City, the Dutch are credited with beginning this practice. Every house was open, and it was considered an insult to skip any friend when making New Year's calls. Appointments or invitations were unnecessary. When leaving a Dutch home on New Year's Day, guests broke off a piece of a "sharing cake" near the front door. This was a way to take home a part of the host's hospitality.

Special houses were noted for particular treats. At one it would be eggnog, at another rum punch, and at another pickled oysters. Staple menu items were honeycakes and *olykoeks* (doughnuts). In later years, champagne became a staple.

Native Americans also celebrated the arrival of the New Year, though not always in January. For the Creek Indians, when the corn ripened in July or August, it signified the end of one year and the beginning of another. It was customary for them at this time to obtain new clothes, furniture, and household goods to replace the old. The old things, along with uneaten food and grain, were set on fire. All the fires in the village were extinguished, then rekindled from the holy fire built by the chief priest.

Methodist colonists are said to have originated Watch Night services in church on New Year's Eve—December 31. The first Watch Night gathering was held at St. George's Methodist Church in Philadelphia in 1770. The services were designed to produce a thoughtful frame of mind concerning the New Year.

Enslaved African-Americans also got together on New Year's Eve for their own, informal, Watch Night observance. They did this because slaveholders typically added up their business accounts on the first day of January. If they found they needed money, they might very well sell some of their slaves. The last night of December was perhaps the last time enslaved families and friends would be together before being separated because of a sale.

English colonists added the turkey shoot to New Year's Day festivities. They also introduced the custom of shooting off guns on New Year's Day. A group would gather and start shooting their guns. As they went from house to house, men from each household would join the group, until the group was quite large.

Sometimes colonial New Year's celebrations became rowdy. The Marquis de Chastellux, a major general who fought with George Washington during the Revolutionary War, recorded one unpleasant incident. At four in the morning on New Year's Day, he was awakened by the sound of a musket firing close to his window. Fifteen minutes later he heard more shots, followed shortly by a loud jumble of voices crying out New Year's greetings. The tired Marquis admitted, "This manner of proclaiming [the New Year] was not . . . very pleasing to me,"[1] but he decided to wait it out, hoping the people would eventually go away. After another thirty minutes, the crowd outside his window had grown to about 100. They fired muskets, knocked rudely at the door, and threw stones against his window. In the morning, he learned that it was customary for these rabble-rousers to go from house to house drinking and

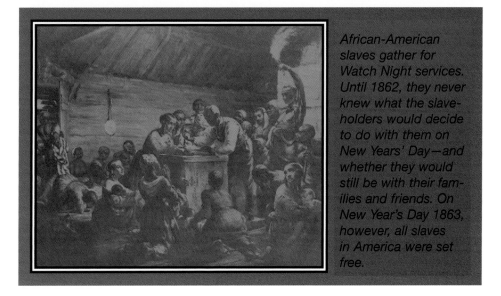

African-American slaves gather for Watch Night services. Until 1862, they never knew what the slaveholders would decide to do with them on New Years' Day—and whether they would still be with their families and friends. On New Year's Day 1863, however, all slaves in America were set free.

demanding money. After he left his room, he said, "I met nobody but drunken people in the streets."[2]

Plow Monday

Plow Monday had been celebrated in Europe, but it was merely observed by most colonial farmers. Traditionally Plow Monday was the first Monday following January 6 ("Twelfth Night," the end of the Christmas holiday), and it marked the beginning of the early farming season. In England, plowmen decorated their plows and went from door to door in costumes, begging for gifts. There were parades of decorated plows through villages. However, most colonial American farmers used Plow Monday as merely the signal to get back to work.

First Skating Day

First Skating Day was the day when the ponds were first frozen in winter. School was canceled, and children and their parents spent the day skating along the frozen surfaces. Once observed in New York State by Dutch settlers, First Skating Day is no longer celebrated.

Candlemas Day

February 2 was Candlemas. Besides being a Christian feast day, celebrated with candles blessed by the church, Candlemas was thought to have significance for farmers. According to tradition, if Candlemas was clear and sunny, it meant there would be forty more days of winter and ultimately poor crops. Medieval people thought that some hibernating animals came to the surface of the ground on Candlemas morning to observe the weather. If the hedgehog (or badger in Germany) saw his shadow—because the weather was pleasant—he crawled back into his hole, and the farmers would expect more cold weather. Early German settlers brought this superstition to America. Since they did not find badgers in the colonies, they used the next best thing—the groundhog.

Valentine's Day

Valentine's Day was not widely celebrated in colonial America. Public displays of affection, at least in New England, were rare and often punished. For example, a Boston sea captain who had just returned from a three-year sea voyage kissed his wife in public and was promptly sentenced to two hours in the stocks.

Settlers who did celebrate Valentine's Day made homemade Valentine's cards decorated with lace, ribbons, and hearts. Sometimes they included poems or clever verses. However, after 1723, the colonists often used valentine "writers," which were booklets imported from England containing numerous verses and messages that could be copied onto decorative paper.

Shrovetide

The Dutch celebrated Shrovetide—the three days, including Shrove Tuesday, just before Ash Wednesday, which Roman Catholics observed as the first day of Lent. It became customary in the colonies to stage cock-fights on Shrove Tuesday. In areas settled by Germans, Shrove Tuesday was called Fastnacht (Eve of the Feast). In England, rich foods were used to make Shrovetide pancakes; in America, these became Fastnachts—rectangular doughnuts.

Lent

Lent, a period of forty days (not including Sundays) between Ash Wednesday and Easter, was celebrated by many colonists. The word *Lent* comes from the word *lencten*, which means "spring." In England, fasting was decreed for Lent, and people were forbidden from having meat, eggs, and milk. By the time the Puritans arrived in America, the fasting practices had been relaxed.

St. Patrick's Day

St. Patrick is the patron saint of Ireland, and St. Patrick's Day has been celebrated in that country for hundreds of years. Supposedly, the first celebration of St. Patrick's Day in colonial America took place in Boston in 1737 by the Protestant Charitable Irish Society of Boston. This was an organization founded that year to help weak or sickly Irishmen. In 1757, English troops celebrated St. Patrick's Day at Fort William Henry on Lake George, New York. That night, a French army attacked the fort, hoping to catch the garrison still celebrating. However, the French were defeated.

The Colonial Army also celebrated St. Patrick's Day. In 1778, an extra ration of grog was issued to the army in honor of the day. At Morristown in 1780, Washington issued an order authorizing the celebration of the day.

April Fool's Day

Early English settlers brought the custom of April fooling to America. It was a day for children, who usually lived a strict life, to have some fun at an adult's expense. Typical tricks kids played included pinning signs on people's backs that said Kick Me or Punch Me; putting pepper or salt in candy; placing a brick under an old hat for someone to stub his toe on when he kicked the hat; and tying a purse on a string, placing it on the street, and then pulling it away when a person bent down to pick it up.

Simnel Sunday

Simnel Sunday was held on the fourth Sunday of Lent. It was also called Mothering Day. This was a holiday for apprentices and house girls to visit their mothers and bring them a Simnel cake. Traditional Simnel cakes had candied violets as a topping.

Easter

Easter was another Christian holiday not widely celebrated in the colonies. The Dutch, however, started a few traditions that have lasted into modern times, such as scratching designs like tulips and butterflies onto eggs. They colored the eggs with dyes made from spinach water, beet juice, onion skins, and tree bark.

Pinkster (Pentecost)

Pinkster was a major holiday for the Dutch. *Pinkster* is a variation of the Dutch word *Pinksteren*, meaning "Pentecost." Pentecost is a Christian feast falling on the seventh Sunday after Easter, but Pinkster would last for several days.

To the Dutch, Pinkster was many things: a chance to rest, gather, celebrate religious services like baptisms and confirmations, and a celebration of the change of seasons and spring renewal. It became a time for feasting and visiting. Neighbors visited with one another and ate soft waffles while children colored eggs and ate sweets like gingerbread. The Dutch traveled in buggies decked with flowers as they visited their neighbors. Pink or purple azaleas replaced the tulips that had been used in their homeland.

For their African slaves, Pinkster was also a holiday. When black families were sold and split up, members might be separated by great distances. Pinkster was a chance for them to meet and catch up with family and friends and to enjoy temporary independence. It also allowed slaves to pass on African culture and traditions, particularly to those born in North America.

Pinkster was also an opportunity for blacks to earn and spend their own money. Merchants decorated their stalls and carts with greenery and flowers, especially azaleas, and then hired skillful black dancers to attract attention to their stalls to advertise sales of berries, herbs, sassafras bark, beverages, and oysters.

May Day

May Day had long been celebrated in various cultures as a signal of the returning flowers and greening of the earth after the bleak, brown days of winter. While some settlers in colonial America celebrated May Day, it was not observed with the enthusiasm that it had been in Europe. Perhaps this was because in 1628, the Puritans from Plymouth sent a military party to cut down a maypole at nearby Mount Merry and punish all those who were drinking and dancing around it.

But some colonists did celebrate May Day. They went "a-maying"— going out early in the morning and gathering flowers. They decorated a tall pole—the maypole—with ribbons and flowers and then danced and sang around it. Another custom was for young girls to gather spring flowers, which they would leave in baskets on the doorstep for their parents.

Celebrations of the Iroquois

The Iroquois were actually a group of five (later six) tribes: the Mohawk, Onondaga, Cayuga, Seneca, and Oneida (joined later by the Tuscaroras). In colonial times, they were the dominant Native American people along the Eastern Seaboard and all the way west to the Mississippi River. The Iroquois had six ceremonies of thanksgiving each year to give thanks to the good spirits for health, clothes, food, and happiness.

The festival year began with the Mid-Winter Festival, which occurred in January or February and lasted about nine days. Next came the Thanks-to-the-Maple celebration in late March, during which people left their villages to camp near family-owned maple groves. When it was time to plant corn in May or June, they held a Corn Planting Festival. At the Strawberry Festival in June, groups of women and children had picnic parties and went out to gather strawberries. The four-day Green Corn Ceremony marking the middle of the year took place in August or September when the corn was ready for picking. October brought the Harvest Festival. At two of these festivals (Mid-Winter and Green Corn), names were chosen for the tribe's infants.

A modern Iroquois dancer

The Iroquois began their New Year in either January, February, or March with a "festival of dreams." These ceremonies lasted several days or even weeks. It was a time when most any type of behavior was tolerated. Often, men and women wearing disguises went around breaking objects and otherwise acting strangely. They were supposedly out of their senses, and thus not responsible for their actions. Many took the opportunity to get revenge on their enemies by drenching them with ice-cold water or covering them with ashes. The only way of escaping was to guess what the disguised person had dreamed about.

One day of the festival was devoted to a ceremony to drive away evil spirits from the village. Men in animal skins, their faces covered with masks, went from hut to hut making awful noises. In every hut they scattered the embers and ashes from the fire onto the floor with their hands.

Women and children in 1959 carry candles to celebrate St. Lucia's Day. One of the primary themes of St. Lucia's Day is light. The word Lucia comes from the Latin word lux, which means "light." This is one reason the holiday occurs around the shortest day of the year—because in the days that follow, the sun's light gets stronger.

Chapter

4

Holidays from July to December

Holidays in colonial America tended to occur less frequently in the second half of the year. There was no national celebration of Thanksgiving, and Christmas was celebrated differently—if at all—depending upon where one lived.

Independence Day

In Philadelphia on July 4, 1777, Independence Day celebrations included ringing bells, lighting bonfires, and shooting fireworks. Ships in the harbor fired thirteen-gun salutes, and houses in the city displayed candles in the windows. The only objection came from the Quakers, who complained when windows were broken during the celebration.

Lammas Day

Lammas Day, celebrated on August 1, marked the first harvest of the year. As such it became the logical day for a thanksgiving celebration, and so it remained among some colonial farming families until the coming of a national Thanksgiving Day many decades later. On Lammas Day the farming family attended church. The head of the household brought with him the first loaf of new-grain bread to be blessed. That loaf was used as the center of a thanksgiving feast.

Harvest Home

Harvest Home was another holiday that enjoyed much greater popularity in England than in America, where it was not widely observed. Harvest Home, which was held on the autumnal equinox, was a time of rest after the crops were gathered in preparation for winter. Villagers joined together to bring the last loads of grain from the fields. Once the work was done, a feast was held. Villages in England would nominate a maiden as Queen of the Harvest, dress her in white, and have her ride atop a loaded cart. Another custom was to make a figure from the grain itself. A white robe was put on this figure, and it was set in a circle of rejoicing farmers.

Harvest Home celebrations were often fun for everyone. For some reason, the holiday was not widely observed in colonial America.

Halloween

Halloween was another day barely noticed in the colonies. However, Irish settlers brought to America two Halloween customs that have continued to modern times—the jack o' lantern and playing pranks. Colonists who did celebrate the day marked it with parties, at which they played games, pulled taffy, and went on hayrides.

Guy Fawkes Day/Gunpowder Plot Day/Pope's Day

When is a holiday not a holiday? The holiday observed on November 5 is an example of celebrating bigotry and intolerance instead of celebrating something positive.

The day was supposed to mark the failure of the infamous Gunpowder Plot in England in 1605. Instead it became a day to heap scorn and abuse on Catholics and the Catholic religion. The "celebration" consisted of settlers' parading through town carrying dummies dressed like the Pope or Catholic priests. At the end of the night, the dummies were thrown into a bonfire.

The main center of "holiday" activity seems to have been in Boston. In the 1730s or even earlier, Boston's craftsmen marked the day with a parade and elaborate dramatic performances mocking the Catholic Pope. For several years, workers from the North End of Boston dominated the day, but South Enders soon began competing with them. What began as friendly competition turned into gang battles marked by violence and death. The victorious group won the right to carry the opposition's pageantry to the top of a hill and burn it. As the years passed, both areas formed paramilitary organizations that participated in the competition with increasingly violent results.

Along with the parade and burnings, Boston's Guy Fawkes Day was a day when the social order was reversed. The young and lower class controlled the streets of town, and went from house to house to demand money to pay for their eating and drinking. Few people thought it safe to refuse their requests.

Thanksgiving

The Pilgrims and Indians held a thanksgiving day in the early autumn of 1621. Thanksgiving days were not new to the Puritans. These early settlers celebrated three types of holy days: the Sabbath (every Sunday), a Day of Humiliation and Fasting, and a Day of Thanksgiving and Praise. A fasting day was called whenever conditions in their community were bad. A thanksgiving day was called whenever conditions were good, for they believed God was pleased.

The Puritans had endured a brutal first winter in America. Of the *Mayflower*'s 102 passengers, 47 had died. When the following autumn came, there was much to be thankful for: people had survived, and the harvest had been successful.

At that 1621 thanksgiving, which lasted three days, food included venison, duck, goose, seafood, eels, pumpkins, corn, white bread, corn bread, leeks, watercress, and a variety of other greens. (Turkey may or may not have been served.) Ninety Native Americans joined the feast, bringing five deer. Wild plums and dried berries were served for dessert. Two people ate from each trencher, a wooden plate with a hollowed-out center about 12 inches square. Four Englishwomen and two teenage girls did the cooking. (Thirteen other Pilgrim women had died over the winter.)

After dinner came the entertainment. There were races, other athletic contests, and stool ball, a type of croquet. Instead of bullets, blanks were fired from guns, and bugles were sounded.

On July 30, 1623, the Pilgrims held a second Thanksgiving to show gratitude to God for saving their crops by sending rain.

Many people feel that these two Puritan celebrations were the first thanksgivings in America. However, a straight line cannot be drawn from any of these celebrations to today's American Thanksgiving holiday.

Thanksgiving actually took root much more slowly in colonial America. Connecticut proclaimed a thanksgiving in 1639 and 1644, and one for every year from 1649 onward. In the Massachusetts Bay Colony, Thanksgiving was held most years after 1660. Plymouth colonists declared their own Thanksgiving whenever they wanted until 1693, when they began going along with the general proclamation of Thanksgiving issued for Massachusetts Bay. Gradually other New England states also began issuing Thanksgiving proclamations, and the day grew in importance by the late seventeenth century. Visiting friends, skating, parlor games, ball games, and a larger feast became parts of the day. Churches eliminated afternoon services so that people would have more time for dinner. By the first years of the eighteenth century, the governors of Connecticut, Massachusetts, and New Hampshire annually proclaimed an autumn thanksgiving. During the American Revolution, the Continental Congress proclaimed several different days of thanksgiving to honor victories won on the battlefield. Thanksgiving Day became fixed on the fourth Thursday in November in 1941.

St. Lucia's Day

Swedish settlers in Delaware celebrated St. Lucia's Day on December 13. People carrying lighted candles paraded through town, led by a young girl dressed as St. Lucia. The light stood for the returning sun, and longer days ahead. The settlers also told stories about Scandinavian gift-givers (red-capped elves with long beards).

Forefathers' Day

Forefathers' Day noted the first landing of the Pilgrims on the shores of Plymouth Bay, Massachusetts. The Old Colony Club of Plymouth held the first Forefathers' Day on December 22, 1769. They had food—pudding, clams, oysters, venison, eel, apple pie, cranberry tarts, and cheese. They also had speeches, odes to Plymouth Rock, songs, and cannon shots. The club held such celebrations for the next three years, but as war loomed, the club disbanded.

Christmas

What some call the first Christmas celebration in America occurred in 1608 in the Virginia colony. Captain John Smith and his men, who were traveling among the Native Americans, had endured a week of brutal wind, rain, and snow. On Christmas, the men were more than ready to relax and celebrate. Smith reported that they "were never more merry, nor fed on more plentie of good Oysters, Fish, Flesh, Wild-foule, and good bread; nor never had better fires in England."[1]

In 1680, a traveler who stopped at a Virginia home on Christmas reported that wine and other beverages flowed freely, and that there was a lot of celebrating. The owner of the home entertained his guests with fiddlers, a jester, a tightrope walker, and an acrobat.

There was no one specific way to celebrate Christmas, and a home that was gay and lively one year might be dark and quiet the next. In 1709 a plantation owner named William Byrd celebrated Christmas by having friends over for a roast beef dinner and revelry. The following year he spent Christmas alone, reading a sermon.

Nevertheless, Christmas celebrations spread throughout Virginia. By the middle of the eighteenth century, the reputation of Virginia Christmases was known in England. In 1746, *London Magazine* reported: "All over the Colony, a universal Hospitality reigns," with "full Tables and open Doors, the kind salute, the generous Detention."[2] For two or three weeks, from the middle of December to Twelfth Night (January 6), the typical Virginia country gentleman celebrated.

Virginians often decorated their houses for Christmas. They made wreaths of spruce, apples, and pinecones, set off by shiny yellow lemons. Indoors they stuffed bits of holly behind paintings and mirrors and used fluffy cottonballs as pretend snow.

31

Holiday meals at the homes of wealthy Virginia plantation owners were large and elaborate. In Williamsburg, a typical holiday table had a cone-shaped centerpiece composed of apples topped with a pineapple, all sitting in a bed of holly. Another popular design was to use a mixture of small lady apples, pinecones, and boxwood to make an X around a soup tureen and four candlesticks.

A big event in Virginia Christmas celebrations was carrying the yule log in from outside and placing it in the fireplace. A bit of the previous year's yule log (which had been kept under a bed) was used to start the new one burning. Throwing a holly sprig into the fire was supposed to end a person's troubles for that year.

In 1773, Philip Vickers Fithian, a tutor at a Virginia plantation called Nomini Hall, recorded the Christmas activities there. Holiday excitement started building on December 18, when, following a British tradition, students prevented one of Fithian's colleagues from teaching until Twelfth Night. Thereafter, all anyone talked about was dancing, foxhunting, parties, and good fellowship.

On Christmas Day itself, the servants at Nomini Hall greeted him by saying, "Joyful Christmas." According to custom, he had to give each servant a few cents. This kept happening until Fithian ran out of money and was forced to give IOUs. As was traditional, guns were shot all around the house.

In contrast, Christmas celebrations in the New England colonies, particularly Massachusetts, got off to a much different start. The Pilgrims aboard the *Mayflower* arrived in Plymouth in December 1620 and spent Christmas Day working. They built "the first house for commone use to receive them and their goods."[3]

But the following year, some members of the colony asked to be excused from working on Christmas Day, saying it went against their conscience to perform labor on that day. Colony Governor William Bradford granted their request. Shortly, however, Bradford was outraged to find these same people playing games in the street. It ran against his conscience, Bradford said, that they should play while others worked. If they wanted to observe Christmas, he said, they would have to stay inside.

The struggle in Massachusetts between those who wanted to celebrate Christmas and those who did not was temporarily decided in 1659 when the Massachusetts Bay General Court banned Christmas. Anyone caught celebrating by "forebearing of labour, feasting, or any other way . . . whosoever shall be found observing any such day as Xmas or the like"[4] would be fined.

In 1681 Massachusetts repealed its ban on Christmas, but the battle continued. Bostonians refused to close their businesses on Christmas Day in 1685 and for years afterward. When urged to honor Christmas, it was pointed out that the Pilgrims had come a long way for religious freedom, and now they were once again being pressured to do something that went against their beliefs.

The middle American colonies were also unable to generate an organized Christmas celebration, but there it was because of the many and varied groups that lived in these areas. In Pennsylvania, for example, Quakers ignored Christmas, while Huguenots, Moravians, Dutch Reformed, and Anglicans all celebrated it in different ways. It was said that Philadelphia could be divided into three categories: those who ignored Christmas, those who wanted to keep Christmas as a strictly religious observance, and those who wanted to celebrate the day with gaiety.

Those who did celebrate Christmas did so with spirit. An account of a 1744 holiday party said that the punch bowl was large enough for six young geese to swim in. Churches that celebrated the holiday decorated their pews and altar with laurel and wound garlands of evergreen around the pulpit.

The Dutch in New Amsterdam (which later became New York City) had no problem with Christmas. They began celebrating on Sinterklaas Eve (St. Nicholas Eve, December 5), and didn't stop until after Christmas Day. Shops were often decorated with bright silk drapes and evergreens. Wives got their homes ready for holiday visitors by polishing the brass, copper, and silver, sanding the floors, and baking enormous amounts of desserts such as *speculaas*, a spicy cookie or biscuit. Houses were decorated with evergreens, which stayed up through Candlemas (February 2).

There were many Dutch traditions associated with the holiday. On Sinterklaas Eve, young people got together to dance, sing, and paste or wrap a gold or silver leaf on small cakes. This was called *koek-plakken*, or cake-pasting. Children waited for the arrival of St. Nicholas, riding his horse. St. Nicholas carried books, cakes, toys, and fruits for youngsters. On St. Nicholas' Eve, every child filled his shoes with hay and a carrot for his horse.

Baking played an important part in the Sinterklaas celebration. Women baked a two-foot-high cookie that resembled St. Nicholas and topped it off with frosting. On Twelfth Night, a special "three kings" bread was baked. It had a bean inside. (Wealthy families put a ring inside.) Whoever got the piece of bread with the bean was king for the night.

Other Twelfth Night customs included having children dance around three candles on the ground, and for adults to go house to house singing, led by three kings, each carrying a pole with a lighted star on the end.

At Christmas, German immigrants who lived around Lancaster, Pennsylvania, believed the Christ Child traveled on mule back throughout the region, leaving gifts on the way. He entered the house through the keyhole. Kids hung stockings or left straw baskets or soup plates on the dining table. Families there built Christmas cribs. They placed straw on the stable floor and arranged animals in a manger.

Christmas parties in colonial America were often called "frolicking." Different regions had different customs. In the New England countryside, revelers entered houses and made a speech. Another popular custom was hanging mistletoe or a "kissing bough" made from evergreen and ribbon. It was customary to slip a tiny sprig of mistletoe into party invitations to wish guests good fortune in the coming year. On Christmas Eve, many colonial families told stories, played cards, danced, and played games like blindman's bluff. Another popular custom was carrying around a wassail bowl—full of spiced ale, sugar, and apples—and singing carols.

Colonial families who lived far away from others traveled to nearby fur trading posts to celebrate Christmas. Sometimes Native Americans joined them.

In Pennsylvania, mumming became popular during the holiday season. Mumming came from an old English tradition. Members of a household, including servants, put on masks and darkened their faces with soot. Sometimes they dressed as animals or even exchanged clothes with one another. Disguised, they played tricks on one another, or went from house to house and entered without permission. Once inside they might sing, dance, or put on a performance of some type.

This custom of mumming was brought to America. Colonists, particularly in Pennsylvania and New York, usually skipped the performance and concentrated on disguises, noisy good humor, and rampaging through neighborhoods. The mummers shot off guns, paraded with musical instruments, and went from house to house in elaborate disguises, begging for food and drink.

When the mummers arrived at a home, it was proper to ask them inside and give them mulled cider, small beer, and homemade cakes. Sometimes the leading mummers were given a bit of money. Even if they were recognized, mummers were never supposed to be called by any name other than the name of the characters they were playing.

34

The Gunpowder Plot

In 1603, James I, a non-Catholic, became King of England. Although at first it seemed he would treat Catholics fairly, James actually turned out to be hard on them. He encouraged the popular feeling that Catholics were traitors to England. (This came about because of England's split with the Catholic Church during the reign of King Henry VIII.) Robert Catesby, an English Catholic, hatched a plot to blow up the king and the House of Lords at the next opening of Parliament. They hoped their revolt would return Catholicism to England.

In May 1604, the growing group of conspirators recruited a man named Guy Fawkes to their cause. He was an adventurer who had fought in the Spanish Army and was used to dangerous situations. Initially the group started to dig a tunnel under the Houses of Parliament, but they abandoned it because it was taking so long. In March 1605, a member of the group rented a cellar right under the House of Lords. Fawkes filled it with 36 barrels of gunpowder. Everything was set for the opening of Parliament on November 5.

Bates.   R. Winter.   C. Wright.   J. Wright.   Percy.   Fawkes.   Catesby.   T. Winter.

Guy Fawkes and the Gunpowder Plotters

Then a member of the House of Lords received an unsigned letter warning him to stay away from the opening session of Parliament. On November 4, the gunpowder was discovered. All the conspirators were eventually captured. The plot had failed. Many unanswered questions about the whole affair, such as who sent the mysterious letter, linger to this day.

The foiling of the gunpowder plot was the event that led to the so-called holiday of Guy Fawkes Day. Catholics and the Catholic religion were not well thought of in some parts of colonial America, helping an observance like Guy Fawkes Day take root.

In a time when entertainment choices were few, court proceedings provided colonial Americans with the chance to socialize . . . and to see if any of their friends were in legal trouble!

Chapter

5

Colonial Celebrations

Besides holidays, colonial Americans also celebrated on other occasions. Some of these may not seem appropriate to people today as celebrations, but life was hard for those in colonial times, and they had to seek entertainment and socializing wherever they could find them.

Fairs

Colonial fairs were usually held once or twice a year, in spring and fall. They often lasted three to ten days. Fairs mixed business and pleasure for the settlers. Farmers sold produce and cattle at agricultural fairs. Entertainment included puppets, tightrope walkers, jugglers, and fiddlers. Activities included bowling, boat races, riding the merry-go-round, playing games, and participating in contests such as whistling, grinning, singing, and wrestling. Two popular contests involved trying to catch a running goose, or a pig with a greased tail. Often prizes were given at fairs for the finest products of the community.

Tug-of-war teams were also prominent entertainment at fairs. Every village, fire brigade, police department, and merchant's association had its own tug-of-war team.

Court Days

In a time without many entertainment choices, court days often provided amusement for colonial Americans. Many people attended the trials of fellow colonists. Punishment usually took place in public because of the belief that the main objective of punishment was public humiliation. Sometimes, court days were combined with other activities. For example, Williamsburg held two Public Times each year. On these days, farmers attended meetings of the General Court and conducted business. They also went to fairs, parties, plays, and horse races.

A man in a pillory. It was hoped that the notion of being punished in full view of everyone was so humiliating that it would prevent people from committing crimes. It didn't always work.

Election Days

Election Days were also sources of celebration. People listened to speeches and debates. Candidates for office often supplied drinks. Frequently food booths were set up too.

Training Days

On Training Days, all young men of military age were required to attend musters, or groups assembled for military purposes. Each township usually held six Training Days per year. The men marched to a drumbeat, rode horses, shot at targets, and participated in other military drills in a festive atmosphere. Children bought penny candy and lemonade. After the drills, the men went to taverns for refreshments.

Commencement Days

Commencement (graduation) days at colonial colleges, such as William and Mary, Yale, and Harvard, were considered times of celebration. In Cambridge, Massachusetts (home of Harvard), festivities could last four or five days. Kegs of beer and tables of food were set out in Harvard Yard for guests, who came from far and wide to hear speakers and drink ale. While few of the participants had any personal relationship with the graduates, the public treasury supported Harvard, so all felt entitled to attend. After-dinner activities included parades, game-playing, singing, building bonfires, and shooting off fireworks.

Births and Baptisms

In a world of hard work, and one in which the specter of death was always present, a birth was always welcome news for colonial Americans. Family members gathered to welcome a new arrival. Sometimes settlers announced the birth of a baby by tying a ribbon to the front door—a blue one for a boy or a white one for a girl.

A baptism was also cause for a party. The Dutch gave an "apostle spoon" to a child on the day he or she was christened. Molded at the end of the handle was the figure of the saint or apostle for whom the child was named. The infant's name and the date were often engraved on the spoon.

Weddings

Just as in modern times, weddings took place either at church or at home. It was customary for the Dutch, who preferred Pinkster as the start of their wedding season, to present a "monkey spoon" to newlyweds. This spoon, representing festivity, had the symbol of a monkey drinking from a goblet and a heart on its handle. Under the figure of the monkey was a likeness of the bridal couple and possibly an engraving of the date.

The night before a wedding, a dance would be held at the house of the bride. Wedding cakes were often baked with a piece of nutmeg inside. Colonists believed that whoever got the nutmeg piece would be the next to marry. The Sunday following the marriage was a special day honoring the bride and groom with singing, dancing, and feasting.

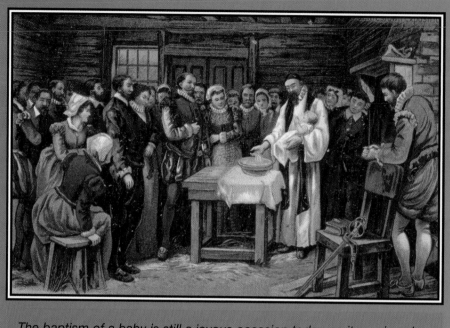

The baptism of a baby is still a joyous occasion today, as it was in colonial times, but in colonial America a baptism also reaffirmed the triumph of the spirit of life in a world that sometimes seemed full of death.

Funerals

Funerals during the early years in New England were public, even mildly celebratory, social events. After the brief funeral ceremony, the mourners would return to the house of the affected family, where they shared a meal and spiced drinks. It was customary—even for those who could not afford it—to pass out costly gifts to those who attended, such as scarves, gloves, and even gold rings. Funerals became an opportunity to display a family's wealth.

Baking

Seasonal baking was also a form of celebration for colonial Americans. There were commencement cakes, watermelon cakes (made in July with red coloring and raisins), and journey cakes for trips. One popular recipe for a journey cake used neither eggs nor milk, which was seldom transported, but cider. Cakes were often packed in popcorn for traveling, so if the cake was damaged, the cake-smeared popcorn could still be eaten. There were special

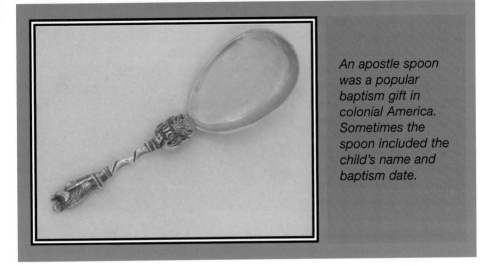

An apostle spoon was a popular baptism gift in colonial America. Sometimes the spoon included the child's name and baptism date.

cakes prepared for Christmas, Easter Eve, Ash Wednesday, and other religious holidays.

Feast Days

Some colonists celebrated the feast day of their favorite saint. The Dutch honored St. Martin's Day each fall with a banquet featuring a special beef and vegetable dish called hodge-podge. On St. Martin's Eve it was believed that ghosts and goblins inhabited the earth. St. Steven's Day was a special occasion for early English settlers, while the French observed St. Catherine's Day. Inhabitants of colonial Williamsburg marked St. George's Day with a fair in the market square.

Charity

Although there was no organized event like a holiday or fair, the first harvest was celebrated in early colonial America as a time of charity. August was the time of the first harvest, and colonial farmers followed the words of the Bible concerning leaving the scraps of the harvest behind for the poor and needy. By custom, a small corner of the field nearest the road was left open (unfenced) for the poor. Usually in the last week of August, a church bell rang or a drum beat, indicating to the poor and needy that they could go to the unfenced fields and collect what they could.

Crime and Punishment in Colonial Times

Colonial justice in America was swift and simple. It was usually open, meaning the public could watch. Judges who handed down punishments had little legal training. They relied upon common sense, experience, and the community environment to deliver a verdict.

In general, first-time offenders received light sentences. The sentences became more severe for repeat offenders. Jail time was usually avoided except for capital crimes. There were several drawbacks to sending someone to jail: The public had to support the prisoner while he served his sentence. He could not support his family while in jail. Finally, locking a person in jail kept the person out of the public's eye and so avoided the chief point of punishment—public humiliation.

However, colonial justice also suffered from double standards. A person's gender and social position determined his or her punishment. Women were treated more harshly than men. A woman who had a child out of wedlock, for instance, could be publicly whipped. All a man had to do was pay a fine and promise to support the child. An ordinary citizen had to serve time in the stocks while sitting; a gentleman could stand.

Colonial courtroom

Courtroom proceedings were often watched by citizens in colonial America. In a world in which entertainment was scarce, watching people was considered an agreeable way to pass the time—and what better place to see friends and neighbors than in a courtroom? Watching legal proceedings was like looking through a giant window into the community: A person might see friends or neighbors come before the judge, or just meet them as part of the general audience of spectators.

Chapter Notes

Chapter 1
Like Any Other Day

1. David Freeman Hawke, *Everyday Life in Early America* (New York, Harper & Row, Publishers, 1988), p. 91.

Chapter 3
Holidays from January to June

1. Robert J. Myers, *Celebrations—The Complete Book of American Holidays* (Garden City, New York, Doubleday and Company, Inc., 1972), p. 9.
2. Ibid., p. 10.

Chapter 4
Holidays from July to December

1. Penne L. Restad, *Christmas In America* (New York, Oxford University Press, 1995), p. 8.
2. Ibid., p. 12.
3. Ibid., p. 8.
4. Ibid, p. 14.

Chronology

1499	Italian navigator Amerigo Vespucci sights the coast of South America.
1507	The name America (after Vespucci) is used for the first time to refer to the New World.
1541	Hernando de Soto of Spain discovers the Mississippi River.
1565	The first permanent European colony in North America is founded by the Spanish at St. Augustine, Florida.
1584	Sir Walter Raleigh lands on Roanoke Island and names the area Virginia.
1587	After multiple attempts, Roanoke Colony is established. By 1590 all the settlers have mysteriously disappeared.
1587	The first English child to be born in America, Virginia Dare, is born in Roanoke on August 18.
1606	The London Company sponsors an expedition to Virginia.
1607	Jamestown is founded in Virginia.
1613	A Dutch trading post is established on Manhattan Island.
1616	A smallpox epidemic decimates the Native American population in New England.
1619	Twenty Africans are brought by a Dutch ship to Jamestown for sale as indentured servants. This is the precursor to slavery in colonial America.
1620	The *Mayflower* lands at Cape Cod, Massachusetts.
1626	Peter Minuit, a Dutch colonist, buys Manhattan island from Native Americans for 60 guilders (about $24) and names it New Amsterdam.
1634	Two hundred colonists settle in Maryland.
1636	Roger Williams founds Rhode Island.
1663	King Charles II establishes the colony of Carolina and grants the territory to eight loyal supporters.

Chronology (cont'd)

1664 The Dutch colony of New Netherland becomes English New York after Peter Stuyvesant surrenders to the British following a naval blockade.

1675–1676 King Philip's War erupts in New England between colonists and Native Americans as a result of tensions over colonist's expansionist activities. The bloody war rages up and down the Connecticut River Valley in Massachusetts and in the Plymouth and Rhode Island colonies, eventually resulting in 600 English colonials and 3,000 Native Americans being killed, including women and children on both sides.

1682 Pennsylvania is founded by William Penn.

1688 Quakers in Pennsylvania issue a formal protest against slavery in America.

1692 Hysteria grips the village of Salem, Massachusetts, as witchcraft suspects are arrested and imprisoned or sentenced to death.

1700 The Anglo population in the English colonies in America reaches 250,000.

1706 Benjamin Franklin is born in Boston on January 17.

1712 The Carolina colony is officially divided into North Carolina and South Carolina.

1720 The population of American colonists reaches 475,000. Boston (pop. 12,000) is the largest city, followed by Philadelphia (pop. 10,000) and New York (pop. 7,000).

1729 Benjamin Franklin begins publishing *The Pennsylvania Gazette*, which eventually becomes the most popular colonial newspaper.

1732 George Washington is born in Virginia.

1743 The American Philosophical Society is founded in Philadelphia by Ben Franklin and his associates.

1752 The first general hospital in the colonies is founded, in Philadelphia.

1754–1763 The Seven Years' War, or the French and Indian War, takes place.

1755 English General Edward Braddock arrives in Virginia with two regiments of English troops. In April, Gen. Braddock and Lt. Col. George Washington set out with nearly 2,000 men to battle the French in the Ohio territory. In July, a force of about 900 French and Indians defeat those English forces. Braddock is mortally wounded.

1760 The population of colonists in America reaches 1,500,000.

1763 The French and Indian War ends with the Treaty of Paris. Under the treaty, France gives England all French territory east of the Mississippi River, except New Orleans. The Spanish give up east and west Florida to the English in return for Cuba.

1776 The colonies declare independence from Great Britain.

Calendar of Colonial Holidays

January
- New Year's Day
- Twelfth Night
- Plow Monday
- First Skating Day (in Dutch New Amsterdam only)
- Mid-Winter Festival (Iroquois; held January or February)

February
- Candlemas Day (Groundhog Day)
- Valentine's Day
- Thanks-to-the-Maple Celebration (Iroquois)

March
- Shrovetide
- Lent
- St. Patrick's Day
- Festival of Dreams (Iroquois New Year, celebrated January, February, or March)

April
- April Fool's Day
- Simnel Sunday
- Easter

May
- May Day
- Pinkster (Pentecost)
- Corn-Planting Festival (Iroquois; held May or June)

June
- Strawberry Festival (Iroquois)

July
- Independence Day (begun in 1777)

August
- Lammas Day
- Charity Harvest (after the first harvest)
- Green Corn Ceremony (Iroquois; held August or September)

September
- Harvest Home

October
- Harvest Festival (Iroquois)
- Halloween

November
- Guy Fawkes Day
- Thanksgiving Day (unofficial holiday; not necessarily celebrated in November)

December
- Sinterklaas Eve (Dutch)
- St. Lucia's Day
- Forefathers' Day
- Christmas
- Watch Night

45

Further Reading

For Young Adults

Asimov, Issac. *The Shaping of North America from Earliest Times to 1763*. Boston: Houghton Mifflin, 1973.

Ingraham, Leonard W. *An Album of Colonial America*. New York: Franklin Watts, 1969.

Lizon, Karen Helene. *Colonial American Holidays and Entertainment*. New York: Franklin Watts, 1993.

Perl, Lila. *Slumps, Grunts, and Snickerdoodles: What Colonial America Ate and Why*. New York: Houghton Mifflin/Clarion Books, 1975.

Smith, Carter, editor. *Daily Life: A Sourcebook on Colonial America*. Brookfield, Connecticut: Millbrook Press, 1991.

————. *The Explorers and Settlers: A Sourcebook on Colonial America*. Brookfield, Connecticut: Millbrook Press, 1991.

Speare, Elizabeth George. *Life in Colonial America*. New York: Random House, 1963.

Wright, Louis B. *Everyday Life in Colonial America*. New York: Putnam, 1965.

Works Consulted

Applebaum, Diana Karter. *Thanksgiving—An American Holiday, An American History*. New York: Facts on File Publications, 1984.

Cohen, Hennig, and Tristram Potter Coffin. *America Celebrates*. Detroit, Michigan: Visible Ink Press, 1991.

Cure, Karen. *An Old-Fashioned Christmas*. New York: Harry N. Abrams, Inc., 1984.

Greif, Martin. *The Holiday Book*. New York: The Main Street Press, 1978.

Hawke, David Freeman. *Everyday Life in Early America*. New York: Harper & Row, Publishers, 1988.

Krythe, Maymie R. *All About American Holidays*. New York, Harper & Brothers, 1962.

Myers, Robert J. *Celebrations—The Complete Book of American Holidays*. Garden City, New York: Doubleday and Company, Inc., 1972.

Restad, Penne L. *Christmas in America*. New York: Oxford University Press, 1995.

Sloane, Eric. *The Seasons of America Past*. New York: Promontory Press, 1988.

Wright, Louis B. *The Cultural Life of the American Colonies 1607–1763*. New York: Harper and Brothers, 1957.

On the Internet

America's Story: Colonial America (1492–1763)
http://www.americaslibrary.gov/cgi-bin/page.cgi/jb/colonial

Colonial America
http://members.aol.com/TeacherNet/Colonial.html

Colonial America from Exploration to American Revolution
http://www.usgennet.org/usa/topic/colonial

Colonial Hall: Biographies of America's Founding Fathers
http://www.colonialhall.com

Schooling, Education, and Literacy in Colonial America
http://alumni.cc.gettysburg.edu/~s330558/schooling.html

Glossary

Anglicans
(ANG-lih-kins)
Members of the Church of England.

apprentice
(uh-PREN-tis)
A person who works with another in order to learn a trade.

baptism
(BAP-tizm)
A ceremony involving water that welcomes a new member to a Christian church.

capital crime
(CAA-pih-tul CRYM)
A crime that is punishable by death.

cockfight
(KOK-fyt)
A fight between gamecocks, which are types of roosters specially bred to fight.

culture
(KUL-chur)
A way of living, passed down from one generation to another.

Dutch Reformed
A group of Christian Protestants who base their religion on the teachings of John Calvin.

gibbous moon
(GIH-bus moon)
The moon when more than half, but not the whole, disk is lit.

grog
A mixture of alcoholic liquor and water.

Huguenots
(HYOO-guh-nots)
Members of a Protestant religious group in France in the sixteenth and seventeenth centuries.

inhospitable
(in-hos-PIH-tih-bul)
Unwelcoming.

kindle
(KIN-dul)
To build or fuel a fire.

lady apple
A tiny sweet-tart apple that can range in color from brilliant red to yellow.

Methodist
(MEH-thuh-dist)
A branch of the Protestant faith.

Moravians
(muh-RAY-vee-ins)
Members of a Protestant religious group from Moravia, formerly part of Austria and now part of the Czech Republic.

morris dancers
(MOR-is dan-sers)
People who perform a costumed folk dance from northern England.

pare
(PAYR)
To remove the outer covering by peeling.

pillory
(PIH-luh-ree)
A wooden frame on a post with holes for the hands and neck in which those guilty of minor offenses were locked as punishment.

Quakers
(KWAY-kurs)
Members of the Religious Society of Friends.

small beer
Beer that contains less alcohol than regular beer.

stocks
A wooden frame on a post with holes for the ankles and sometimes the wrists in which those guilty of minor offenses were locked as punishment.

spouse
A husband or wife.

wassail
(WAH-sul or wah-SAYL)
To drink to someone's good health; also, a hot, spiced cider or wine, often containing baked apples, served especially at Christmas.

Index